Introduction

Timeless advice for living a life of prosperity and meaning. Like precious gems -small, brilliant, enduring, valuable and as rare as common sense -these quotes can help you create the best version of yourself.

I loved how Uncle Joe always had a way to twist a phrase to get a point across. He was an inspector at a factory that made circuit breakers. A shop steward and active in his union, he went to work every day. He wasn't lavish by any means. Uncle Joe was a regular guy who developed his hobby of investing. He gave it his time and his energy and in return, it gave him money.

I've met people in my workshops that knew uncle Joe and put their kids through college on his investment ideas. I can remember how he explained dividends to me when I was only six years old.

Uncle Joe could be counted on in times of difficulty and not just because he had money. Because he had money, money was never the issue. He had time to go for a walk with people and talk and listen to them about the real problem. Uncle Joe gave advice with humor and without giving lectures. He never forced his ideas on anyone but he never wavered just because the truth became inconvenient. He gave his advice by example, and by invitation.

He understood life as well as money.

"Done is better than perfect." -Uncle Joe

Beginning Your Day

What does this quote mean to me personally today?

_____

_____

_____

How can I apply this quote today?

_____

_____

_____

Who else needs to hear this quote today?

_____

_____

_____

At the End of Your Day

How did I apply this quote today?

_____

_____

_____

What will I do differently going forward?

_____

_____

_____

"When the student is ready, the teacher will appear." - Lao Tzu

Beginning Your Day

What does this quote mean to me personally today?

_____

_____

_____

How can I apply this quote today?

_____

_____

_____

Who else needs to hear this quote today?

_____

_____

_____

At the End of Your Day

How did I apply this quote today?

_____

_____

_____

What will I do differently going forward?

_____

_____

_____

"Believe you can and you're halfway there."
-Theodore Roosevelt

Beginning Your Day

What does this quote mean to me personally today?

_____

_____

_____

How can I apply this quote today?

_____

_____

_____

Who else needs to hear this quote today?

_____

_____

_____

At the End of Your Day

How did I apply this quote today?

_____

_____

_____

What will I do differently going forward?

_____

_____

_____

"Thousands of candles can be lighted from a single candle, and the life of that candle will not be shortened. Happiness never decreases by being shared." -The Buddah

Beginning Your Day

What does this quote mean to me personally today?

_____

_____

_____

How can I apply this quote today?

_____

_____

_____

Who else needs to hear this quote today?

_____

_____

_____

At the End of Your Day

How did I apply this quote today?

_____

_____

_____

What will I do differently going forward?

_____

_____

_____

"Direction is more important than speed." -Uncle Joe

Beginning Your Day

What does this quote mean to me personally today?

_____

_____

_____

How can I apply this quote today?

_____

_____

_____

Who else needs to hear this quote today?

_____

_____

_____

At the End of Your Day

How did I apply this quote today?

_____

_____

_____

What will I do differently going forward?

_____

_____

_____

"The minute you start compromising for the sake of massaging somebody's ego, that's it, game over." -Gordon Ramsay

Beginning Your Day

What does this quote mean to me personally today?

_____

_____

_____

How can I apply this quote today?

_____

_____

_____

Who else needs to hear this quote today?

_____

_____

_____

At the End of Your Day

How did I apply this quote today?

_____

_____

_____

What will I do differently going forward?

_____

_____

_____

"Our ambition should be to rule ourselves, the true kingdom for each one of us; and true progress is to know more, and be more, and to do more." -Oscar Wilde

Beginning Your Day

What does this quote mean to me personally today?

_____

_____

_____

How can I apply this quote today?

_____

_____

_____

Who else needs to hear this quote today?

_____

_____

_____

At the End of Your Day

How did I apply this quote today?

_____

_____

_____

What will I do differently going forward?

_____

_____

_____

"The first hour of every day is yours to keep." -Uncle Joe

Beginning Your Day

What does this quote mean to me personally today?

_____

_____

_____

How can I apply this quote today?

_____

_____

_____

Who else needs to hear this quote today?

_____

_____

_____

At the End of Your Day

How did I apply this quote today?

_____

_____

_____

What will I do differently going forward?

_____

_____

_____

"You miss 100% of the shots you don't take."
-Wayne Gretzky

Beginning Your Day

What does this quote mean to me personally today?

_____

_____

_____

How can I apply this quote today?

_____

_____

_____

Who else needs to hear this quote today?

_____

_____

_____

At the End of Your Day

How did I apply this quote today?

_____

_____

_____

What will I do differently going forward?

_____

_____

_____

"If you really want to do something, you will find a way. If you don't, you'll find an excuse." -Jim Rohn

Beginning Your Day

What does this quote mean to me personally today?

_____

_____

_____

How can I apply this quote today?

_____

_____

_____

Who else needs to hear this quote today?

_____

_____

_____

At the End of Your Day

How did I apply this quote today?

_____

_____

_____

What will I do differently going forward?

_____

_____

_____

"I like nonsense, it wakes up the brain cells. Fantasy is a necessary ingredient in living, it's a way of looking at life through the wrong end of a telescope. Which is what I do, and that enables you to laugh at life's realities."" -Dr. Seuss

Beginning Your Day

What does this quote mean to me personally today?

_____

_____

_____

How can I apply this quote today?

_____

_____

_____

Who else needs to hear this quote today?

_____

_____

_____

At the End of Your Day

How did I apply this quote today?

_____

_____

_____

What will I do differently going forward?

_____

_____

_____

"Success is not final, failure is not fatal; it is courage to continue that counts." -Winston Churchill

Beginning Your Day

What does this quote mean to me personally today?

_____

_____

_____

How can I apply this quote today?

_____

_____

_____

Who else needs to hear this quote today?

_____

_____

_____

At the End of Your Day

How did I apply this quote today?

_____

_____

_____

What will I do differently going forward?

_____

_____

_____

"The lion doesn't lose sleep over the opinion of sheep" -Uncle Joe

Beginning Your Day

What does this quote mean to me personally today?

_____

_____

_____

How can I apply this quote today?

_____

_____

_____

Who else needs to hear this quote today?

_____

_____

_____

At the End of Your Day

How did I apply this quote today?

_____

_____

_____

What will I do differently going forward?

_____

_____

_____

"I've missed more than 9,000 shots in my career. I've lost almost 300 games. 26 times I've been trusted to take the game winning shot and missed. I've failed over and over and over again in my life and that is why I succeed." -Michael Jordan

Beginning Your Day

What does this quote mean to me personally today?

_____

_____

_____

How can I apply this quote today?

_____

_____

_____

Who else needs to hear this quote today?

_____

_____

_____

At the End of Your Day

How did I apply this quote today?

_____

_____

_____

What will I do differently going forward?

_____

_____

_____

"There is nothing in a caterpillar that can tell you it's going to be a butterfly." -Buckminster Fuller

Beginning Your Day

What does this quote mean to me personally today?

_____

_____

_____

How can I apply this quote today?

_____

_____

_____

Who else needs to hear this quote today?

_____

_____

_____

At the End of Your Day

How did I apply this quote today?

_____

_____

_____

What will I do differently going forward?

_____

_____

_____

"Being rich is a good thing. Not just in the obvious sense of benefitting you and your family, but in the broader sense. Profits are not a zero sum game. The more you make, the more of a financial impact you can have." -Mark Cuban

Beginning Your Day

What does this quote mean to me personally today?

_____

_____

_____

How can I apply this quote today?

_____

_____

_____

Who else needs to hear this quote today?

_____

_____

_____

At the End of Your Day

How did I apply this quote today?

_____

_____

_____

What will I do differently going forward?

_____

_____

_____

"You have to get good at one of two things: Planting in the Spring or begging in the Fall." -Jim Rohn

Beginning Your Day

What does this quote mean to me personally today?

_____

_____

_____

How can I apply this quote today?

_____

_____

_____

Who else needs to hear this quote today?

_____

_____

_____

At the End of Your Day

How did I apply this quote today?

_____

_____

_____

What will I do differently going forward?

_____

_____

_____

"The first step to get out of a hole is to stop digging." -Uncle Joe

Beginning Your Day

What does this quote mean to me personally today?

_____

_____

_____

How can I apply this quote today?

_____

_____

_____

Who else needs to hear this quote today?

_____

_____

_____

At the End of Your Day

How did I apply this quote today?

_____

_____

_____

What will I do differently going forward?

_____

_____

_____

"Nothing happens suddenly when you're paying attention. Everything is a surprise when you're not." -George McReynolds

Beginning Your Day

What does this quote mean to me personally today?

_____

_____

_____

How can I apply this quote today?

_____

_____

_____

Who else needs to hear this quote today?

_____

_____

_____

At the End of Your Day

How did I apply this quote today?

_____

_____

_____

What will I do differently going forward?

_____

_____

_____

"When saying 'yes' to others, make sure you aren't saying 'no' to yourself." -Paulo Coehlo

Beginning Your Day

What does this quote mean to me personally today?

_____

_____

_____

How can I apply this quote today?

_____

_____

_____

Who else needs to hear this quote today?

_____

_____

_____

At the End of Your Day

How did I apply this quote today?

_____

_____

_____

What will I do differently going forward?

_____

_____

_____

"Strong minds discuss ideas, average minds discuss events, weak minds discuss people." -Socrates

Beginning Your Day

What does this quote mean to me personally today?

_____

_____

_____

How can I apply this quote today?

_____

_____

_____

Who else needs to hear this quote today?

_____

_____

_____

At the End of Your Day

How did I apply this quote today?

_____

_____

_____

What will I do differently going forward?

_____

_____

_____

"Let us always meet each other with a smile, for the smile is the beginning of love." -Mother Teresa

Beginning Your Day

What does this quote mean to me personally today?

_____

_____

_____

How can I apply this quote today?

_____

_____

_____

Who else needs to hear this quote today?

_____

_____

_____

At the End of Your Day

How did I apply this quote today?

_____

_____

_____

What will I do differently going forward?

_____

_____

_____

"Tell me and I forget. Teach me and I remember. Involve me and I learn." -Benjamin Franklin

Beginning Your Day

What does this quote mean to me personally today?

_____

_____

_____

How can I apply this quote today?

_____

_____

_____

Who else needs to hear this quote today?

_____

_____

_____

At the End of Your Day

How did I apply this quote today?

_____

_____

_____

What will I do differently going forward?

_____

_____

_____

"You can't have a better tomorrow if you are always thinking about yesterday." -Charles F. Kettering

Beginning Your Day

What does this quote mean to me personally today?

_____

_____

_____

How can I apply this quote today?

_____

_____

_____

Who else needs to hear this quote today?

_____

_____

_____

At the End of Your Day

How did I apply this quote today?

_____

_____

_____

What will I do differently going forward?

_____

_____

_____

"What you want, wants you." -Uncle Joe

Beginning Your Day

What does this quote mean to me personally today?

_____

_____

_____

How can I apply this quote today?

_____

_____

_____

Who else needs to hear this quote today?

_____

_____

_____

At the End of Your Day

How did I apply this quote today?

_____

_____

_____

What will I do differently going forward?

_____

_____

_____

"Be grateful for what you have and stop complaining. It bores everyone else, does you no good, and doesn't solve any problems." -Zig Ziglar

Beginning Your Day

What does this quote mean to me personally today?

_____

_____

_____

How can I apply this quote today?

_____

_____

_____

Who else needs to hear this quote today?

_____

_____

_____

At the End of Your Day

How did I apply this quote today?

_____

_____

_____

What will I do differently going forward?

_____

_____

_____

"Live as if you were to die tomorrow. Learn as if you were to live forever." -Mahatma Gandhi

Beginning Your Day

What does this quote mean to me personally today?

_____

_____

_____

How can I apply this quote today?

_____

_____

_____

Who else needs to hear this quote today?

_____

_____

_____

At the End of Your Day

How did I apply this quote today?

_____

_____

_____

What will I do differently going forward?

_____

_____

_____

"Prosperity is your ability to trust that the divine will provide and replenish." -Glenn Morshower

Beginning Your Day

What does this quote mean to me personally today?

_____

_____

_____

How can I apply this quote today?

_____

_____

_____

Who else needs to hear this quote today?

_____

_____

_____

At the End of Your Day

How did I apply this quote today?

_____

_____

_____

What will I do differently going forward?

_____

_____

_____

"The measure of who we are is what we do with what we have." -Vince Lombardi

Beginning Your Day

What does this quote mean to me personally today?

_____

_____

_____

How can I apply this quote today?

_____

_____

_____

Who else needs to hear this quote today?

_____

_____

_____

At the End of Your Day

How did I apply this quote today?

_____

_____

_____

What will I do differently going forward?

_____

_____

_____

"Your journey has molded you for your greater good, and it was exactly what it needed to be. Don't think that you've lost time. It took each and every situation you have encountered to bring you to the now. And now is right on time." -Asha Tyson

Beginning Your Day

What does this quote mean to me personally today?

_____
_____
_____

How can I apply this quote today?

_____
_____
_____

Who else needs to hear this quote today?

_____
_____
_____

At the End of Your Day

How did I apply this quote today?

_____
_____
_____

What will I do differently going forward?

_____
_____
_____

"You can save your way into poverty but you can't spend your way into prosperity." -Uncle Joe

Beginning Your Day

What does this quote mean to me personally today?

_____

_____

_____

How can I apply this quote today?

_____

_____

_____

Who else needs to hear this quote today?

_____

_____

_____

At the End of Your Day

How did I apply this quote today?

_____

_____

_____

What will I do differently going forward?

_____

_____

_____

"Strive not to be a success, but rather to be of value." -Albert Einstein

Beginning Your Day

What does this quote mean to me personally today?

_____

_____

_____

How can I apply this quote today?

_____

_____

_____

Who else needs to hear this quote today?

_____

_____

_____

At the End of Your Day

How did I apply this quote today?

_____

_____

_____

What will I do differently going forward?

_____

_____

_____

"There is little success where there is little laughter." -Andrew Carnegie

Beginning Your Day

What does this quote mean to me personally today?

_____

_____

_____

How can I apply this quote today?

_____

_____

_____

Who else needs to hear this quote today?

_____

_____

_____

At the End of Your Day

How did I apply this quote today?

_____

_____

_____

What will I do differently going forward?

_____

_____

_____

"If you hear a voice within you say 'you cannot paint,' then by all means, paint, and that voice will be silenced." -Vincent Van Gogh

Beginning Your Day

What does this quote mean to me personally today?

_____

_____

_____

How can I apply this quote today?

_____

_____

_____

Who else needs to hear this quote today?

_____

_____

_____

At the End of Your Day

How did I apply this quote today?

_____

_____

_____

What will I do differently going forward?

_____

_____

_____

"It's not what you make. It's what you keep that counts." -Uncle Joe

Beginning Your Day

What does this quote mean to me personally today?

_____

_____

_____

How can I apply this quote today?

_____

_____

_____

Who else needs to hear this quote today?

_____

_____

_____

At the End of Your Day

How did I apply this quote today?

_____

_____

_____

What will I do differently going forward?

_____

_____

_____

"Money and success don't change people; they merely amplify what is already there." -Will Smith

Beginning Your Day

What does this quote mean to me personally today?

_____

_____

_____

How can I apply this quote today?

_____

_____

_____

Who else needs to hear this quote today?

_____

_____

_____

At the End of Your Day

How did I apply this quote today?

_____

_____

_____

What will I do differently going forward?

_____

_____

_____

"I'd rather regret the things I've done, than regret the things I haven't done." -Lucille Ball

Beginning Your Day

What does this quote mean to me personally today?

_____

_____

_____

How can I apply this quote today?

_____

_____

_____

Who else needs to hear this quote today?

_____

_____

_____

At the End of Your Day

How did I apply this quote today?

_____

_____

_____

What will I do differently going forward?

_____

_____

_____

"Don't let the fear of striking out hold you back." -Babe Ruth

Beginning Your Day

What does this quote mean to me personally today?

_____

_____

_____

How can I apply this quote today?

_____

_____

_____

Who else needs to hear this quote today?

_____

_____

_____

At the End of Your Day

How did I apply this quote today?

_____

_____

_____

What will I do differently going forward?

_____

_____

_____

"It's better to be approximately right than precisely wrong." -Uncle Joe

Beginning Your Day

What does this quote mean to me personally today?

_____

_____

_____

How can I apply this quote today?

_____

_____

_____

Who else needs to hear this quote today?

_____

_____

_____

At the End of Your Day

How did I apply this quote today?

_____

_____

_____

What will I do differently going forward?

_____

_____

_____

"Happiness is not something you postpone for the future; it is something you design for the present." -Jim Rohn

Beginning Your Day

What does this quote mean to me personally today?

_____

_____

_____

How can I apply this quote today?

_____

_____

_____

Who else needs to hear this quote today?

_____

_____

_____

At the End of Your Day

How did I apply this quote today?

_____

_____

_____

What will I do differently going forward?

_____

_____

_____

"The only way to permanently change the temperature in the room is to reset the thermostat. In the same way, the only way to change your level of financial success 'permanently' is to reset your financial thermostat. But it is your choice whether you choose to change." -T. Harv Eker

Beginning Your Day

What does this quote mean to me personally today?

_____
_____
_____

How can I apply this quote today?

_____
_____
_____

Who else needs to hear this quote today?

_____
_____
_____

At the End of Your Day

How did I apply this quote today?

_____
_____
_____

What will I do differently going forward?

_____
_____
_____

"Be yourself; everyone else is already taken." -Oscar Wilde

Beginning Your Day

What does this quote mean to me personally today?

_____

_____

_____

How can I apply this quote today?

_____

_____

_____

Who else needs to hear this quote today?

_____

_____

_____

At the End of Your Day

How did I apply this quote today?

_____

_____

_____

What will I do differently going forward?

_____

_____

_____

"I do not fix problems. I fix my thinking. The problems fix themselves." -Louise Hay

Beginning Your Day

What does this quote mean to me personally today?

_____

_____

_____

How can I apply this quote today?

_____

_____

_____

Who else needs to hear this quote today?

_____

_____

_____

At the End of Your Day

How did I apply this quote today?

_____

_____

_____

What will I do differently going forward?

_____

_____

_____

"A successful man will profit from his mistakes and try again in a different way" -Dale Carnegie

Beginning Your Day

What does this quote mean to me personally today?

_____

_____

_____

How can I apply this quote today?

_____

_____

_____

Who else needs to hear this quote today?

_____

_____

_____

At the End of Your Day

How did I apply this quote today?

_____

_____

_____

What will I do differently going forward?

_____

_____

_____

"Success isn't pursued, it's attracted by becoming the person you want to be." -Jim Rohn

Beginning Your Day

What does this quote mean to me personally today?

_____

_____

_____

How can I apply this quote today?

_____

_____

_____

Who else needs to hear this quote today?

_____

_____

_____

At the End of Your Day

How did I apply this quote today?

_____

_____

_____

What will I do differently going forward?

_____

_____

_____

"Progress is impossible without change, and those who cannot change their minds cannot change anything." -George Bernard Shaw

Beginning Your Day

What does this quote mean to me personally today?

_____

_____

_____

How can I apply this quote today?

_____

_____

_____

Who else needs to hear this quote today?

_____

_____

_____

At the End of Your Day

How did I apply this quote today?

_____

_____

_____

What will I do differently going forward?

_____

_____

_____

"Life is a series of experiences, each one of which makes us bigger, even though sometimes it is hard to realize this. For the world was built to develop character, and we must learn that the setbacks and grieves which we endure help us in our marching onward." -Henry Ford

Beginning Your Day

What does this quote mean to me personally today?

_____

_____

_____

How can I apply this quote today?

_____

_____

_____

Who else needs to hear this quote today?

_____

_____

_____

At the End of Your Day

How did I apply this quote today?

_____

_____

_____

What will I do differently going forward?

_____

_____

_____

"You can't borrow your way out of debt." -Uncle Joe

Beginning Your Day

What does this quote mean to me personally today?

_____

_____

_____

How can I apply this quote today?

_____

_____

_____

Who else needs to hear this quote today?

_____

_____

_____

At the End of Your Day

How did I apply this quote today?

_____

_____

_____

What will I do differently going forward?

_____

_____

_____

"Sometimes if you want to see a change for the better, you have to take things into your own hands." -Clint Eastwood

Beginning Your Day

What does this quote mean to me personally today?

_____

_____

_____

How can I apply this quote today?

_____

_____

_____

Who else needs to hear this quote today?

_____

_____

_____

At the End of Your Day

How did I apply this quote today?

_____

_____

_____

What will I do differently going forward?

_____

_____

_____

"The road to hell was paved with good intentions." -Your Mother

Beginning Your Day

What does this quote mean to me personally today?

_____

_____

_____

How can I apply this quote today?

_____

_____

_____

Who else needs to hear this quote today?

_____

_____

_____

At the End of Your Day

How did I apply this quote today?

_____

_____

_____

What will I do differently going forward?

_____

_____

_____

"The beginning is the most important part of the work." -Plato

Beginning Your Day

What does this quote mean to me personally today?

_____

_____

_____

How can I apply this quote today?

_____

_____

_____

Who else needs to hear this quote today?

_____

_____

_____

At the End of Your Day

How did I apply this quote today?

_____

_____

_____

What will I do differently going forward?

_____

_____

_____

"Nothing is impossible, the word itself says 'I'm possible'!" -Audrey Hepburn

Beginning Your Day

What does this quote mean to me personally today?

_____

_____

_____

How can I apply this quote today?

_____

_____

_____

Who else needs to hear this quote today?

_____

_____

_____

At the End of Your Day

How did I apply this quote today?

_____

_____

_____

What will I do differently going forward?

_____

_____

_____

"If your actions inspire others to dream more, learn more, do more and become more, you are a leader." -John Quincy Adams

Beginning Your Day

What does this quote mean to me personally today?

_____

_____

_____

How can I apply this quote today?

_____

_____

_____

Who else needs to hear this quote today?

_____

_____

_____

At the End of Your Day

How did I apply this quote today?

_____

_____

_____

What will I do differently going forward?

_____

_____

_____

"I have found the paradox, that if you love until it hurts, there can be no more hurt, only more love."
-Mother Teresa

Beginning Your Day

What does this quote mean to me personally today?

_____

_____

_____

How can I apply this quote today?

_____

_____

_____

Who else needs to hear this quote today?

_____

_____

_____

At the End of Your Day

How did I apply this quote today?

_____

_____

_____

What will I do differently going forward?

_____

_____

_____

"You need better ways to save, not better ways to spend." -Uncle Joe

Beginning Your Day

What does this quote mean to me personally today?

_____

_____

_____

How can I apply this quote today?

_____

_____

_____

Who else needs to hear this quote today?

_____

_____

_____

At the End of Your Day

How did I apply this quote today?

_____

_____

_____

What will I do differently going forward?

_____

_____

_____

"Mystery creates wonder and wonder is the basis of man's desire to understand." -Neil Armstrong

Beginning Your Day

What does this quote mean to me personally today?

_____
_____
_____

How can I apply this quote today?

_____
_____
_____

Who else needs to hear this quote today?

_____
_____
_____

At the End of Your Day

How did I apply this quote today?

_____
_____
_____

What will I do differently going forward?

_____
_____
_____

"In wisdom gathered over time I have found that every experience is a form of exploration." -Ansel Adams

Beginning Your Day

What does this quote mean to me personally today?

_____

_____

_____

How can I apply this quote today?

_____

_____

_____

Who else needs to hear this quote today?

_____

_____

_____

At the End of Your Day

How did I apply this quote today?

_____

_____

_____

What will I do differently going forward?

_____

_____

_____

"If you think the price of education is high, you should see the price of ignorance"." -Uncle Joe

Beginning Your Day

What does this quote mean to me personally today?

_____

_____

_____

How can I apply this quote today?

_____

_____

_____

Who else needs to hear this quote today?

_____

_____

_____

At the End of Your Day

How did I apply this quote today?

_____

_____

_____

What will I do differently going forward?

_____

_____

_____

"The size of your success is measured by the strength of your desire; the size of your dream; and how you handle disappointment along the way." -Robert Kiyosaki

Beginning Your Day

What does this quote mean to me personally today?

_____

_____

_____

How can I apply this quote today?

_____

_____

_____

Who else needs to hear this quote today?

_____

_____

_____

At the End of Your Day

How did I apply this quote today?

_____

_____

_____

What will I do differently going forward?

_____

_____

_____

"You're going to go through tough times, that's life. But I say, 'Nothing happens *to* you, it happens *for* you.' See the positive in negative events." -Joel Osteen

Beginning Your Day

What does this quote mean to me personally today?

_____

_____

_____

How can I apply this quote today?

_____

_____

_____

Who else needs to hear this quote today?

_____

_____

_____

At the End of Your Day

How did I apply this quote today?

_____

_____

_____

What will I do differently going forward?

_____

_____

_____

"Never mistake motion for action." -Ernest Hemingway

Beginning Your Day

What does this quote mean to me personally today?

_____

_____

_____

How can I apply this quote today?

_____

_____

_____

Who else needs to hear this quote today?

_____

_____

_____

At the End of Your Day

How did I apply this quote today?

_____

_____

_____

What will I do differently going forward?

_____

_____

_____

"No man ever achieved worthwhile success, who did not at one time or another, find himself with at least one foot hanging well over the brink of failure." -Napoleon Hill

Beginning Your Day

What does this quote mean to me personally today?

_____

_____

_____

How can I apply this quote today?

_____

_____

_____

Who else needs to hear this quote today?

_____

_____

_____

At the End of Your Day

How did I apply this quote today?

_____

_____

_____

What will I do differently going forward?

_____

_____

_____

**"What is success? I think it is a mixture of having a flair for the thing that you are doing; knowing that it is not enough, that you have got to have hard work and a certain sense of purpose."
-Margaret Thatcher**

Beginning Your Day

What does this quote mean to me personally today?

_____
_____
_____

How can I apply this quote today?

_____
_____
_____

Who else needs to hear this quote today?

_____
_____
_____

At the End of Your Day

How did I apply this quote today?

_____
_____
_____

What will I do differently going forward?

_____
_____
_____

"I don't believe in circumstances. The people who get on in this world are the people who get up and look for the circumstances they want, and, if they can't find them, make them." -George Bernard Shaw

Beginning Your Day
What does this quote mean to me personally today?

_____

_____

_____

How can I apply this quote today?

_____

_____

_____

Who else needs to hear this quote today?

_____

_____

_____

At the End of Your Day
How did I apply this quote today?

_____

_____

_____

What will I do differently going forward?

_____

_____

_____

"You can't *think* your way out of something you *behaved* your way into." -Uncle Joe

Beginning Your Day

What does this quote mean to me personally today?

_____

_____

_____

How can I apply this quote today?

_____

_____

_____

Who else needs to hear this quote today?

_____

_____

_____

At the End of Your Day

How did I apply this quote today?

_____

_____

_____

What will I do differently going forward?

_____

_____

_____

"When your outgo exceeds your income, your upkeep will become your downfall. " -Theodore Halfling

Beginning Your Day

What does this quote mean to me personally today?

_____

_____

_____

How can I apply this quote today?

_____

_____

_____

Who else needs to hear this quote today?

_____

_____

_____

At the End of Your Day

How did I apply this quote today?

_____

_____

_____

What will I do differently going forward?

_____

_____

_____

"We can learn something new anytime we believe we can." -Virginia Satir

Beginning Your Day

What does this quote mean to me personally today?

_____

_____

_____

How can I apply this quote today?

_____

_____

_____

Who else needs to hear this quote today?

_____

_____

_____

At the End of Your Day

How did I apply this quote today?

_____

_____

_____

What will I do differently going forward?

_____

_____

_____

"When values are clear, decisions are easy." -Roy Disney

Beginning Your Day

What does this quote mean to me personally today?

_____

_____

_____

How can I apply this quote today?

_____

_____

_____

Who else needs to hear this quote today?

_____

_____

_____

At the End of Your Day

How did I apply this quote today?

_____

_____

_____

What will I do differently going forward?

_____

_____

_____

"A wise man can learn more from a foolish question than a fool can learn from a wise answer." -Bruce Lee

Beginning Your Day

What does this quote mean to me personally today?

_____

_____

_____

How can I apply this quote today?

_____

_____

_____

Who else needs to hear this quote today?

_____

_____

_____

At the End of Your Day

How did I apply this quote today?

_____

_____

_____

What will I do differently going forward?

_____

_____

_____

The larger portion of the truth arises from the seemingly irrelevant." -Edgar Allan Poe

Beginning Your Day

What does this quote mean to me personally today?

_____

_____

_____

How can I apply this quote today?

_____

_____

_____

Who else needs to hear this quote today?

_____

_____

_____

At the End of Your Day

How did I apply this quote today?

_____

_____

_____

What will I do differently going forward?

_____

_____

_____

"It's not what you pay, it's what you get that counts." -Uncle Joe

Beginning Your Day

What does this quote mean to me personally today?

_____

_____

_____

How can I apply this quote today?

_____

_____

_____

Who else needs to hear this quote today?

_____

_____

_____

At the End of Your Day

How did I apply this quote today?

_____

_____

_____

What will I do differently going forward?

_____

_____

_____

"The road to happiness is paved with good decisions." -George McReynolds

Beginning Your Day

What does this quote mean to me personally today?

_____

_____

_____

How can I apply this quote today?

_____

_____

_____

Who else needs to hear this quote today?

_____

_____

_____

At the End of Your Day

How did I apply this quote today?

_____

_____

_____

What will I do differently going forward?

_____

_____

_____

"To effectively communicate, we must realize that we are all different in the way we perceive the world and use this understanding as a guide to our communication with others." -Tony Robbins

Beginning Your Day

What does this quote mean to me personally today?

_____

_____

_____

How can I apply this quote today?

_____

_____

_____

Who else needs to hear this quote today?

_____

_____

_____

At the End of Your Day

How did I apply this quote today?

_____

_____

_____

What will I do differently going forward?

_____

_____

_____

"Don't find fault, find a remedy." -Henry Ford

Beginning Your Day

What does this quote mean to me personally today?

_____

_____

_____

How can I apply this quote today?

_____

_____

_____

Who else needs to hear this quote today?

_____

_____

_____

At the End of Your Day

How did I apply this quote today?

_____

_____

_____

What will I do differently going forward?

_____

_____

_____

"If you don't know where you're going, you could end up someplace else." -Uncle Joe

Beginning Your Day

What does this quote mean to me personally today?

_____

_____

_____

How can I apply this quote today?

_____

_____

_____

Who else needs to hear this quote today?

_____

_____

_____

At the End of Your Day

How did I apply this quote today?

_____

_____

_____

What will I do differently going forward?

_____

_____

_____

"It's not over until you win." -Les Brown

Beginning Your Day

What does this quote mean to me personally today?

_____

_____

_____

How can I apply this quote today?

_____

_____

_____

Who else needs to hear this quote today?

_____

_____

_____

At the End of Your Day

How did I apply this quote today?

_____

_____

_____

What will I do differently going forward?

_____

_____

_____

"Do the one thing you think you cannot do. Fail at it. Try again. Do better the second time. The only people who never tumble are those who never mount the high wire. This is your moment. Own it." -Oprah Winfrey

Beginning Your Day

What does this quote mean to me personally today?

_____

_____

_____

How can I apply this quote today?

_____

_____

_____

Who else needs to hear this quote today?

_____

_____

_____

At the End of Your Day

How did I apply this quote today?

_____

_____

_____

What will I do differently going forward?

_____

_____

_____

"Change your thoughts and you change your world." -Norman Vincent Peale

Beginning Your Day

What does this quote mean to me personally today?

_____

_____

_____

How can I apply this quote today?

_____

_____

_____

Who else needs to hear this quote today?

_____

_____

_____

At the End of Your Day

How did I apply this quote today?

_____

_____

_____

What will I do differently going forward?

_____

_____

_____

"If you're going through hell, don't stop. Keep going." -Uncle Joe

Beginning Your Day

What does this quote mean to me personally today?

_____

_____

_____

How can I apply this quote today?

_____

_____

_____

Who else needs to hear this quote today?

_____

_____

_____

At the End of Your Day

How did I apply this quote today?

_____

_____

_____

What will I do differently going forward?

_____

_____

_____

"Everything you really want is downstream."
-Donna Enstrom

Beginning Your Day

What does this quote mean to me personally today?

_____

_____

_____

How can I apply this quote today?

_____

_____

_____

Who else needs to hear this quote today?

_____

_____

_____

At the End of Your Day

How did I apply this quote today?

_____

_____

_____

What will I do differently going forward?

_____

_____

_____

"I have learned over the years that when one's mind is made up, that diminishes fear; knowing what must be done does away with fear." -Rosa Parks

Beginning Your Day

What does this quote mean to me personally today?

_____

_____

_____

How can I apply this quote today?

_____

_____

_____

Who else needs to hear this quote today?

_____

_____

_____

At the End of Your Day

How did I apply this quote today?

_____

_____

_____

What will I do differently going forward?

_____

_____

_____

"Our greatest weakness lies in giving up. The most certain way to succeed is always to try just one more time." -Thomas A. Edison

Beginning Your Day

What does this quote mean to me personally today?

_____

_____

_____

How can I apply this quote today?

_____

_____

_____

Who else needs to hear this quote today?

_____

_____

_____

At the End of Your Day

How did I apply this quote today?

_____

_____

_____

What will I do differently going forward?

_____

_____

_____

"The starting point of all achievement is desire." -Napoleon Hill

Beginning Your Day

What does this quote mean to me personally today?

_____

_____

_____

How can I apply this quote today?

_____

_____

_____

Who else needs to hear this quote today?

_____

_____

_____

At the End of Your Day

How did I apply this quote today?

_____

_____

_____

What will I do differently going forward?

_____

_____

_____

"Who chooses the road also chooses the outcome."
-Lao Tzu

Beginning Your Day

What does this quote mean to me personally today?

_____

_____

_____

How can I apply this quote today?

_____

_____

_____

Who else needs to hear this quote today?

_____

_____

_____

At the End of Your Day

How did I apply this quote today?

_____

_____

_____

What will I do differently going forward?

_____

_____

_____

"Whatever you are, be a good one." -Abraham Lincoln

Beginning Your Day

What does this quote mean to me personally today?

_____

_____

_____

How can I apply this quote today?

_____

_____

_____

Who else needs to hear this quote today?

_____

_____

_____

At the End of Your Day

How did I apply this quote today?

_____

_____

_____

What will I do differently going forward?

_____

_____

_____

"Any man who reads too much and uses his own brain too little falls into lazy habits of thinking." -Albert Einstein

Beginning Your Day

What does this quote mean to me personally today?

_____

_____

_____

How can I apply this quote today?

_____

_____

_____

Who else needs to hear this quote today?

_____

_____

_____

At the End of Your Day

How did I apply this quote today?

_____

_____

_____

What will I do differently going forward?

_____

_____

_____

**"If you are the kind of person who is waiting for the 'right' thing to happen, you might wait for a long time. It's like waiting for all the traffic lights to be green for five miles before starting the trip."
-Robert Kiyosaki**

Beginning Your Day
What does this quote mean to me personally today?

_____

_____

_____

How can I apply this quote today?

_____

_____

_____

Who else needs to hear this quote today?

_____

_____

_____

At the End of Your Day
How did I apply this quote today?

_____

_____

_____

What will I do differently going forward?

_____

_____

_____

"The people that give the most advice have the least knowledge and the loudest voices." -Uncle Joe

Beginning Your Day

What does this quote mean to me personally today?

_____

_____

_____

How can I apply this quote today?

_____

_____

_____

Who else needs to hear this quote today?

_____

_____

_____

At the End of Your Day

How did I apply this quote today?

_____

_____

_____

What will I do differently going forward?

_____

_____

_____

"If we are not a little bit uncomfortable every day, we're not growing. All the good stuff is outside our comfort zone." -Jack Canfield

Beginning Your Day

What does this quote mean to me personally today?

_____

_____

_____

How can I apply this quote today?

_____

_____

_____

Who else needs to hear this quote today?

_____

_____

_____

At the End of Your Day

How did I apply this quote today?

_____

_____

_____

What will I do differently going forward?

_____

_____

_____

"If a man empties his purse into his head, no man can take it away from him. An investment in knowledge always pays the best interest."
-Benjamin Franklin

Beginning Your Day

What does this quote mean to me personally today?

_____

_____

_____

How can I apply this quote today?

_____

_____

_____

Who else needs to hear this quote today?

_____

_____

_____

At the End of Your Day

How did I apply this quote today?

_____

_____

_____

What will I do differently going forward?

_____

_____

_____

"Darkness cannot drive out darkness; only light can do that. Hate cannot drive out hate; only love can do that." -Martin Luther King, Jr.

Beginning Your Day

What does this quote mean to me personally today?

_____

_____

_____

How can I apply this quote today?

_____

_____

_____

Who else needs to hear this quote today?

_____

_____

_____

At the End of Your Day

How did I apply this quote today?

_____

_____

_____

What will I do differently going forward?

_____

_____

_____

"When you practice gratefulness, there is a sense of respect toward others." -Dalai Lama

Beginning Your Day

What does this quote mean to me personally today?

_____

_____

_____

How can I apply this quote today?

_____

_____

_____

Who else needs to hear this quote today?

_____

_____

_____

At the End of Your Day

How did I apply this quote today?

_____

_____

_____

What will I do differently going forward?

_____

_____

_____

"Hardships often prepare ordinary people for an extraordinary destiny." -C.S. Lewis

Beginning Your Day

What does this quote mean to me personally today?

_____
_____
_____

How can I apply this quote today?

_____
_____
_____

Who else needs to hear this quote today?

_____
_____
_____

At the End of Your Day

How did I apply this quote today?

_____
_____
_____

What will I do differently going forward?

_____
_____
_____

"If you pay peanuts, you'll get monkeys." -Uncle Joe

Beginning Your Day

What does this quote mean to me personally today?

_____

_____

_____

How can I apply this quote today?

_____

_____

_____

Who else needs to hear this quote today?

_____

_____

_____

At the End of Your Day

How did I apply this quote today?

_____

_____

_____

What will I do differently going forward?

_____

_____

_____

"I am always doing that which I cannot do, in order that I may learn how to do it." -Pablo Picasso

Beginning Your Day

What does this quote mean to me personally today?

_____

_____

_____

How can I apply this quote today?

_____

_____

_____

Who else needs to hear this quote today?

_____

_____

_____

At the End of Your Day

How did I apply this quote today?

_____

_____

_____

What will I do differently going forward?

_____

_____

_____

"Nothing brings man so much suffering and humility as poverty." -Napoleon Hill

Beginning Your Day

What does this quote mean to me personally today?

_____

_____

_____

How can I apply this quote today?

_____

_____

_____

Who else needs to hear this quote today?

_____

_____

_____

At the End of Your Day

How did I apply this quote today?

_____

_____

_____

What will I do differently going forward?

_____

_____

_____

"Never ask a barber if you need a haircut." - Uncle Joe

Beginning Your Day

What does this quote mean to me personally today?

_____

_____

_____

How can I apply this quote today?

_____

_____

_____

Who else needs to hear this quote today?

_____

_____

_____

At the End of Your Day

How did I apply this quote today?

_____

_____

_____

What will I do differently going forward?

_____

_____

_____

"Measure twice; cut once." -Uncle Joe

Beginning Your Day

What does this quote mean to me personally today?

_____

_____

_____

How can I apply this quote today?

_____

_____

_____

Who else needs to hear this quote today?

_____

_____

_____

At the End of Your Day

How did I apply this quote today?

_____

_____

_____

What will I do differently going forward?

_____

_____

_____

"If you think it's expensive to hire a professional just wait until you hire an amateur." -Uncle Joe

Beginning Your Day

What does this quote mean to me personally today?

_____

_____

_____

How can I apply this quote today?

_____

_____

_____

Who else needs to hear this quote today?

_____

_____

_____

At the End of Your Day

How did I apply this quote today?

_____

_____

_____

What will I do differently going forward?

_____

_____

_____

"Ask not, what your country can do for you; ask what you can do for your country." -John F. Kennedy

Beginning Your Day

What does this quote mean to me personally today?

_____

_____

_____

How can I apply this quote today?

_____

_____

_____

Who else needs to hear this quote today?

_____

_____

_____

At the End of Your Day

How did I apply this quote today?

_____

_____

_____

What will I do differently going forward?

_____

_____

_____

""In the end, the love you take is equal to the love you make." -The Beatles

Beginning Your Day

What does this quote mean to me personally today?

_____

_____

_____

How can I apply this quote today?

_____

_____

_____

Who else needs to hear this quote today?

_____

_____

_____

At the End of Your Day

How did I apply this quote today?

_____

_____

_____

What will I do differently going forward?

_____

_____

_____

Meet George McReynolds

George has been helping successful people with all aspects of their lives and personal finances for the past 35 years.

He is a Certified Financial Fiduciary®, Certified Financial Planner® professional, Registered Financial Consultant and author of the personal finance book, "Prosperity By Design: How to make great financial decisions."

He is also an experienced life coach, certified as a Master Trainer of TQ Time Management, Certified as an NLP Practitioner and board certified as a clinical hypnotherapist. He is also a certified firearms safety instructor.

He is an active public speaker and an often-quoted media resource for personal finance, tax, and real estate topics as well as time management and personal growth. He spoke on the subject of goal setting and visualization at the Expert Summit at *The Harvard Club of Boston* in 2019. His speech was published in the 2020 edition of the book, "Expert Stories". He recently wrote the foreword to the latest edition of the book, "9 Money Mistakes That Doctors Make," written by Dr. Vicki Rackner. He was featured on the cover of Suburban Life Magazine in Philadelphia.

George is a former first responder having served as an MP, EMT (Emergency Medical Technician) & Paramedic and as a SWAT police officer. He received numerous commendations and saved the lives of more than a dozen people using First Aid and CPR.

George is a decorated veteran of the US Army and served on the security detail for the Supreme Allied Commander at NATO headquarters in Belgium. He kept his secret clearance serving with an Intelligence Unit in the Reserves. He graduated with high honors from both the 1st Army Intelligence School and the Military Police School. He was awarded the High Scholastic Award upon graduation from the Pennsylvania State Police Academy.

His rich history of trust, service, courage and protecting the weak and innocent continues in everything he does.

www.ProtectiveWealthcare.com   www.McWealth.com
www.TQCoach.com   www.JustAbundance.com

Made in the USA
Middletown, DE
02 July 2021

43351165R00060